Withered Branches, Broken Pieces

Dom Contreras

Copyright @2022 by Dom Contreras

All rights reserved. No part of this book may be reproduced in any form or by any electronic or mechanical means, including information storage and retrieval systems, without permission in writing from the publisher, except by reviewers, who may quote brief passages in a review.

This publication contains the opinions and ideas of It's author. It is intended to provide helpful and informative material on the subjects addressed in the publication. The author and publisher specifically disclaim all responsibility for any liability, loss or risk, personal or otherwise, which is incurred as a consequence, directly or indirectly, of the use and application of any of the contents of this book.

WORKBOOK PRESS LLC
187 E Warm Springs Rd,
Suite B285, Las Vegas, NV 89119, USA

Website:	https://workbookpress.com/
Hotline:	1-888-818-4856
Email:	admin@workbookpress.com

Ordering Information:
Quantity sales. Special discounts are available on quantity purchases by corporations, associations, and others.
For details, contact the publisher at the address above.

Library of Congress Control Number:

ISBN-13:   978-1-952754-31-9 (Paperback Version)
            978-1-952754-32-6 (Digital Version)

REV. DATE: 09/12/2022

Withered Branches, Broken Pieces

Dom Contreras Ph. D

TABLE OF CONTENTS

Chapter One
    The Sand Dollar   1

Chapter Two
    Sand Castles   5

Chapter Three
    Withered Branches   9

Chapter Four
    Eye of the Storm   13

Chapter Five
    "When God Does a Root Canal"   17

Chapter Six
    Lessons Learned From a Dog   20

Chapter Seven
    Keeping in Step   24

Chapter Eight
  Salt of the Earth   28

Chapter Nine
  Building the Kingdom   31

Chapter Ten
  Hearing the Master's Voice   34

Chapter Eleven
  Surfing the Waves   38

Chapter Twelve
  The Early Fig   42

Chapter Thirteen
  Light Bulbs Come in All Sizes   46

Chapter Fourteen
  Grace With Age   49

Chapter Fifteen
  More Precious Than Gold   54

Chapter Sixteen
> Lost and Found   59

Chapter Seventeen
> Road Signs   63

Chapter Eighteen
> Behind Closed Doors   66

Chapter Nineteen
> Mountain Climbing   70

Chapter Twenty
> "Greco Roman Style"   74

Chapter Twenty-One
> Needed Foot Washing   79

Chapter Twenty-Two
> "Father to the Fatherless"   83

SYNOPSIS

Why I wrote Withered Branches, Broken Pieces book is that, while walking along the sea-shore, I spotted a sand dollar. It had not been eaten by the Sea-Gull. When I got home, I thought about how fragile they are when out of the water environment. This encounter was the incentive for me to write this book. It was also a great learning experience. I learned a great lesson on ecology, all life is precious to God, even a sea urchin like the sand dollar.

ABOUT THE AUTHOR

Dominic Contreras has a Ph.D. in Marriage and Family. He served as a hospital chaplain and worked for various community agencies as an at-risk counselor. He has also overseen several mainly Spanish-speaking churches. He and his wife have four children and several grandkids.

Chapter One

The Sand Dollar

"There is the sea, vast and spacious, teeming with creatures beyond number, living things both large and small."

(Psalms 104:25)

One of my favorite pastimes is to walk by the sea. As I walk along the sandy

Beach, I enjoy meditating and praying, always keeping my eyes open for small nuggets; not mineral gold but seashells, or colored rocks washed and shaped by the pressure of the sea water. Always keeping an eye out for one of God's beauties, a sea urchin, also called a sand dollar.

As I walk along engrossed in my thoughts my mind drifts to some of the scenes from the Bible that is vivid about our Lord as He walked along the Sea of Galilee. I wonder if He looked for the bright colored seashells that lie on the bright white sands of Galilee or perhaps, He stooped to pick up a Sand Dollar.

Once while meandering along, my eye caught sight of one of God's treasures, a Sand Dollar lying on a stretch of open white sand. As I bent over to pick it up, I was enthralled by its size and unique design. Most Sand Dollars have a flower-type design on the hard shell, usually in the shape of a five-leaf flower. What impressed me about this particular sea urchin was that the design was in the shape of a cross. I was so excited about my new-found treasure I could hardly wait to get it home to share the find with my wife. In my haste without thinking I placed the Sand

Dollar in my windbreaker pocket and forgot how fragile they are.

As I continued my walk and meditation my thoughts focused on how wonderful our God is. My thoughts turned to the book of Genesis and how astounding the creation account is described.

So, God created the great creatures of the sea and every living and moving thing with which the water teems, according to their kinds and every winged bird according to its kind. And God saw that it was good.

(Genesis 1:21)

God sees everything He creates as good, even a little sea urchin that for many is insignificant. I often reflect how the smallest creature is so important to our Creator. I was to learn a great life principle in my minute find.

When I arrived home, I reached into my jacket pocket and found mostly sand and fragments of what once was a perfect specimen of a Sand Dollar. There are approximately 130 different species and I had found the perfect example, yet in my haste to preserve this little creature, I destroyed it with my seat belt. Instead of wrapping the dollar in a napkin or placing it next to me on the seat, I shattered it by leaving it in my pocket; the pressure of my seat belt destro9yed the very thing I tried to preserve.

One day while praying the Lord spoke to me in that still voice, did you learn anything from the Sand Dollar? I also heard Him say all life is precious to Him. All life is fragile, especially when taken out of its natural habitat. The Holy Spirit spoke to my heart about how gently He is with all of us, even a small creature from the vast oceans.

His word states,

Let heaven and earth praise Him the seas and all that move in them.

(Psalm 69:34)

I thought even the sea urchins praise Him. Another verse states,

They will summon peoples to the mountain and there offer sacrifices of righteousness; they will feast on the abundance of the seas, on the treasures hidden in the sand.

(Deuteronomy 33:19)

The latter part of this verse is so clear, even an insignificant sea creature is important to God and a treasure.

Each and every thing that God has created is precious in His sight. Jesus said that the sparrow that falls to earth is important to God, the same as a Sand Dollar that lives out its life span in the oceans of the earth.

As I reflected on the verse in Deuteronomy, I am amazed at how God views all life, regardless of it form. In God's ecology all life in priceless. God placed all life on this planet for man to rule over. Man, because of the fall, lost part of the lordship God had given him W have been give a stewardship over the earth but under that stewardship we are held accountable in how we treat all His creation.

When a life is taken out of its environment it is vulnerable to the alien elements it will encounter. A Sand Dollar is safe as long as it is in the ocean. It becomes food for the gulls and other birds that prowl the seashore when washed upon the sand.

Christians are extremely vulnerable when they leave the sanctity of Christian fellowship. We are susceptible to predators that prey on the weak. When believers seek council from ungodly people, they are apt to fall into temptation and can-do irreparable damage to themselves and others. Like the Sand Dollar, we are secure when we are in Christian fellowship, but take us out of our environment and we can be broken, shattered and wounded and gall into great sin. God has created a perfect place for is in His Son, a perfect environment.

Like my seat belt shattered the Sand Dollar, sin that is allowed to dwell in the believer will shatter your life. We are fragile and only a loving caring God can put the pieces back together again.

The next time you go to the seashore and look for those golden nuggets remember, For they shall suck of the abundance of the seas and of treasure hidden in the sand.

(Deuteronomy 33:19b)

You may find that perfect Sand Dollar or seashell, placed there by God just for you.

Chapter Two
Sand Castles

He is like a man building a house that dug down deep and laid the foundation on a rock. When a flood came, the torrent struck that house but could not shake it, because it was well built.

(Luke 6:48)

I remember that as a boy I used to love to go to the seashore and swim in the surf and do all sorts of fun things. One of my favorite things to do was building sandcastles, Going to the beach, as we called it, was a place where we spent the entire day body surfing, the amusement rides, and playing in the sand, building the biggest and tallest sandcastle we could make.

One of the difficulties of building sandcastles is keeping the ocean from washing away what you have constructed. We would dig wall in front and pile the sand as high as we could and hope the tide would hold back until we completed our masterpiece. I remember we would come back the next day and the tide would have destroyed what we toiled all day to construct. At times, a slight trace of a futile attempt by children could be seen.

There are some who build their lives like sandcastles. When adversity strikes their lives crumble, they fall apart just like a sandcastle and whatever they have built washes away.

Jesus stated,

Therefore, everyone who hears these words of mine and puts them into practice is like a wise man who built his house on the rock.

(Matthew 7:24)

Luke said, "He is like a man building a house, who dug down deep and laid the foundation on rock. When a flood came, the torrent struck that house but could not shake it, because it was well built." (Luke 6:48). These two verses describe people who have followed the teachings of Christ.

Lives built on worldly standards will crumble when trial or adversity strikes. Was Jesus referring to Himself as "The Rock?" I believe so since He is referred to as the "Rock" in various passages of scripture. "There is no Rock like our God (I Sam. 2:2b).

David the psalmist describes God as the rock in a special way,

Turn your ear to Me, come quickly to my rescue; be my rock of refuge, a strong fortress to save me. Since you are my rock and my fortress, for the sake of your name lead and guide me.

(Psalms 31:2-3)

David recognized God as his rock of refuge in times of trial, his guide

A sandcastle is a fantasy for children, a replica of a fortress. When you build your life on sandy ground there is no firm foundation. Like a sandcastle, when the first test comes it won't stand up to the trail, all your dreams and plans are washed away with the storms of lie. Note that David said God was his rock and fortress, his place of refuge. What about you: is your faith found on the Rock?

If your Christian foundation is on shaky ground and not rooted in the "Rock," it's time to evaluate where you are. Are you building sandcastles or a firm foundation?

Jesus said,

Therefore, everyone who hears these words of mine and puts them into practice is like a wise man who built his house on the rock. The rain came down, the streams rose, and the winds blew and beat against that house: yet it did not fall, because it had its foundation on the rock.

(Matt. 7:24-25)

I still like to go to the seashore and see the children build sandcastles, working hard to keep back the tide that will wash away their hard work. Due to the nature of the tides, since they change and shift daily, the sandcastles will wash away, leaving only a lasting memory of a summer remembered as fun.

Life is like the tides of the sea; in time it washes away the memory of a hurt, a relationship that turned sour. A friend or a parent dies and leaves us with only our memories of them, fading into that final summer of life. These are the true tests of our faith.

Building sandcastles is fun when we are young, because they are created on the seashore. But when we are mature, we need to learn to build our lives on the "Rock" Jesus Christ, not sandcastles. He alone is our foundation. Then when the storms of life come, and they will strike when we least expect them, we then can rest secure in Him, our Rock.

Without warning a furious storm came up on the lake, so that the waves swept over the boat. But Jesus was sleeping.

(Matt. 8:24)

Note that storms come without warning, is not life the same? As a pastor and having dealt with people who are going through a trial, a storm of life, for some it is very obvious they have built their lives on the sand, rather than on the "Rock." Christ is the one who can see us through the storms of life. He is always in the boat with us, and it is only He who can calm the storm.

Building sandcastles are for the young. Building a firm foundation takes commitment; a daily commitment in our lives, living the teachings of Christ, "The Rock."

Chapter Three

Withered Branches

Even if it is transplanted, will it thrive? Will it not wither completely when the east wind strikes it; wither away in the plot where it grew?

(Ezekiel 17:10)

Several years ago, I lived on the eastern side of the Sierra Mountains. One of my daily rituals was to rise early in the morning to walk near the edge of the forest. Each day I would pass a mountain meadow where at one time there was a thriving apply orchard. Each day as I passed the meadow, I was saddened by what I saw. The apple trees that once produced lush fruit had been allowed to lay fallow. Instead of beautiful pruned tees, all you saw was gnarled, withered branches protruding from apply trees that once produced rich fruit.

Apparently, the owners of the orchard felt it was not feasible to grow apples. This part of the country produces great apples because of the cold weather, an ideal climate for apples to thrive.

There were days that I contemplated how they must have looked when they were allowed to produce fruit. In fact, all they needed to produce rich juicy apples was for the trees to be pruned, sprayed and watered.

Once as I walked along praying and meditating, I thought of the following passage of scripture.

I am the true vine, and my Father is the gardener. He cuts off every branch in me that bears no fruit, while every branch that does bear fruit, he prunes so that it will be even more fruitful. You are already clean because of the word I have spoken to you. Remain in me, and I will remain in you. No branch can bear fruit by itself; it must remain in the vine. Neither can you bear fruit unless you remain in me. I am the vine; you are the branches. If a man remains in me and I in him, he will bear much fruit; apart from me you can do nothing. If anyone does not remain in me, he is like a branch that is thrown away and withers; such branches are picked up, thrown into the fire and burned. If you remain in me and my words remain in you, ask whatever you wish, and it will be given you. This is to my Father's glory, that you bear much fruit, showing yourselves to be my disciples.

(John 15:1-8)

As I understand the process of pruning, unless you prune the tree or vine at a specific time of year it is difficult for the tree or the vine to produce healthy fruit. God is that way with His creation – He prunes us at just the right time.

This passage of scripture in the Gospel of John speaks of a vine not a tree, but the process is the same; pruning must take place for the tree or vine to produce fruit that is edible.

We are like the fruit trees and the grapevine; unless we produce fruit, we are thrown into the fire, but God prunes us first so we will produce more fruit.

He cuts off every branch in me that bears no fruit, while every branch that does bear fruit, he prunes so that it will be even more fruitful.

(John 15:2)

My understanding of God's role in all this is that He does the pruning. We do not know when He does it.

How does God prune His creation? When was the last time you were challenged for your core beliefs? Or you went through a trial that stretched you to the limit and caused you grief and anguish. How did you respond to the challenge? This is the way God prunes us, through the trials and tests we encounter in life.

People, whose lives are bleak and dreary, and without joy, remind me of the apple trees whose leaves were withered and gnarled. The apple orchard could have been restored to a productive field. The process of simply pruning them, cutting off all the dead branches would have restored them. God is the master pruner who gently cuts away the dead branches, but in order for us to be pruned by God we must be part of the vine.

Jesus said,

No branch can bear fruit by itself; it must remain in the vine. Neither can you bear fruit unless you remain in me.

(John 15:4b)

In order for us to bear fruit, we, His people, must remain in Christ the Vine. We belong to His body, thus bearing fruit and being pruned becomes a way of life for all believers.

When I see people walking in darkness, their lives one crisis after another, wandering aimlessly, I see those apple trees that were withered, with no life. Yet the potential is there. But first they must come to the Master so that He can prune them. Each individual can reach their potential with

God's tender loving care, restored to product fruit.

God, in His infinite wisdom, gives every soul an opportunity to repent, to be grafted into His Son the true vine, but first He prunes away all the sin, all the blemishes, and starts the process of producing fruit. Where are you in your walk? Do you resist the master Vine-Dresser God or do you let Him prune you? The choice is yours.

Chapter Four

Eye of the Storm

A furious squall came up, and the waves broke over the boat, so that it was early swamped. Jesus was in the stern, sleeping on a cushion. The disciples woke him and said to him, 'Teacher, don't you care if we drown?' He got up, rebuked the wind and said to the waves. 'Quiet! Be still!' Then the wind died down and it was completely calm.

(Mark 4:37-39)

Years ago, when I was a young man, I, along with thousands of other young men, was called to serve my country in the Army during the Korean conflict. I remember so clearly the day we shipped out. We were loaded on a troop ship, four thousand young men going to war. The anticipation of going to a foreign country and not knowing what awaited us added to our anxiety level.

I was a ship the size of two football fields, crammed with soldiers. Most of them had never been away from home; some were frightened with the thought of never returning to our homeland. Other thoughts raced through our minds, such as what would happen to our families, our wives, our sweethearts. Even thought of killing another human preoccupied our minds.

The one thing that is so vivid in my mind was the number of men that could be packed into a compartment. The bunks were stacked six high, with barely enough room to turn over. I am six feet three inches tall and weighed about 185 lbs. When I stretched out, my feet dangled over the edge. I was to spend 12 days in these cramped quarters.

Factor in that most of these men had never been on a ship, or a tossing sea that caused most of us to get seasick. It was not a pleasant experience for most of us, but the worst was yet to come.

After we had been out to sea for about four days the captain announced that we would be hit by the tail end of a typhoon that night. We were told to wear our lifejacket if we were brave enough to venture topside, otherwise we were advised to stay in our quarters.

I remember it was close to midnight when the storm struck. We couldn't hear the wind but the pitch and roll of the vessel made it extremely difficult to stay in the hammock-type bunk. I soon learned the safest place to be was near the fantail (tail end of the ship) in the rest rooms; safe because you could get away from the stench of the men who were seasick.

The most frightening thing about the entire episode was the fear of the waves sinking the ship. Each time the ship would roll and pitch the sound of the props made a horrendous noise, adding to our frightened state of mind. I can still hear the sound they made. A loud banging as the props cleared the water. Imagine hitting a large piece of metal with a sledge hammer, multiplied several hundred times.

Today as I reflect on this experience, I think of our Lord as He slept in the boat and His reaction to the apostles on the Sea of Galilee.

Leaving the crowd behind, they took him along, just as he was, in the boat. There were also other boats with him. A furious squall came up, and the waves broke over the boat, so that it was nearly swamped. Jesus was in the stern, sleeping on a cushion. The disciples woke him and said to him 'Teacher, don't you care if we drown?' He got up, rebuked the wind and said to the waves, "Quiet! Be still!' Then the wind died down and it was completely calm. He said to his disciples, "Why are you so afraid? Do you still have no faith?' They were terrified and asked each other, 'Who is this? Even the wind and the waves obey him!'

(Mark 6:36-41)

I can reflect on the incident above and can relate to the apostles' fears. When I went through my ordeal, I was a nominal believer, in fact somewhat of an agnostic, but I remember praying that if there was a God, He would deliver us from the raging storm.

Like the apostles I had no faith and suffered emotional stress needlessly. We survived the turbulent storm because the captain of the ship was wise in how he guided the vessel. Life at times is like a raging storm or it can be like the waters of a clear lake in the early morning when it is calm, which can become a raging torrent when the wind blows.

Christ was asleep in the boat, but challenged the apostles by His words, "Do you still have no faith?" As long as the waters were smooth, they were willing to trust Him. As long as He created miracles to feed them, they were willing to believe in Him, but when things got rough, they had no faith. Scripture teaches us that we will go through tests.

James says:

Consider it pure joy, my brothers, whenever you face trials of many kinds, because you know that the testing of your faith develops perseverance. Perseverance must finish its work so that you may be mature and complete, not lacking anything.

(James 1:2-4)

Each trial, each testing, every trauma we will encounter in life will make us stronger. Our faith will strengthen us, toughen and hone us for the next challenge that life will bring, but we can rest assured that Jesus is in the boat wit us saying have faith and I will see you through this. I am in the boat with you. Have no fear, put your trust in Me, He states. Or are we like some of Christ's followers that followed Him because of the miracles and the food He provided? Do we trust Him only when like is smooth and all is well, or do we fall away when the sea gets turbulent?

The book of Hebrews states:

And without faith it is impossible to please God, because anyone who comes to him must believe that he exists and that he rewards those who earnestly seek him.

(Hebrews 11:6)

If we are to please God then we must be men and women of faith. "Consequently, faith comes from hearing the message, and the message is heard through the word of God" (Rom. 10:17). The next time you are facing a trial, pick up your Bible and read it to increase your faith.

Chapter Five

"When God Does a Root Canal"

Make sure there is no man or woman, clan or tribe among you today whose heart turns away from the Lord our God to go and worship the gods of those nations; make sure there is no root among you that produces such bitter poison.

(Deuteronomy 29:18)

One of the things I detest, more than all other things I must periodically do, is to go to the dentist. I don't have a problem with having them cleaned, but when it requires drilling, I detest it with a passion. Even worse is having a root canal; believe me I know all about root canals.

I remember one time when we were traveling, establishing ethnic churches. We were in Reno, Nevada speaking at a Spanish church when all of a sudden one of my molars started to ache. The week prior I had undergone a root canal on the same molar.

I completed my sermon and returned to the motel, I had intended to stay overnight, but because of the pain caused by my tooth we left the motel and headed home.

At the time of this ordeal, I was over three hundred miles from the sanctuary of our home. By the time I got home I had lost rack of how many pain pills I had taken, and still the intensity of the pain had increased. Needless to say, it was one of those nights we call a nightmare.

The following morning, I called my dentist to see how soon I could get in to see him. To my dismay he was on vacation, but I could see another dentist on an emergency basis. By this time, I was in such pain a plumber cold have pulled my tooth. I arrived at the dentist's office as soon as the doors opened. He proceeded to tell me that he would have to do the root canal over. This was only the beginning of a three-month ordeal with several visits to numerous different types of specialists.

One of the specialists discovered that the molar was cracked at the roots. He recommended that in order to relieve the pain the tooth needed to be extracted. I lost a main molar but it got rid of my problem

Now each time my tongue touches the empty space I think of the pain and agony of three different root canals and the sleepless nights I suffered with a cracked tooth

Root canals are a necessity for healthy dental hygiene, as when God has to purge sin from our hearts. God rids us of our sins when we confess them, but He warns us in scripture "make sure there is no root among you that produces such bitter poison" (Deuteronomy 29:18). This verse deals with following after other gods, which, in God's kingdom is a sin and needs to be rooted out like a root canal where the roots are killed.

Un-repented sin unless rooted out and allowed to fester, can spread to others. God the Holy Spirit has a tender way of doing root canals. Sometimes they are painful

and at other times you barely notice the pain, but regardless they are essential to a healthy spiritual life.

Next time you're going through a difficult time in your life and God is doing something in your like perhaps He is doing a root canal. Or He may be doing a cleaning. Either way it is spiritual hygiene going on in the believer's life. Cleaning your teeth can at times be uncomfortable, but if it's a root canal it can cause a great deal of discomfort. If sin is a deep-rooted spiritual problem, then only the master dentist can kill the sin. He knows what is best for us, just like in the dentist chair. Don't resist, it may get worse.

Chapter Six

Lessons Learned From a Dog

Like one who seizes a dog by the ears is a passer-by who meddles in a quarrel not his own.

(Proverbs 26:17)

Everyone loves to hold a cuddly puppy. They smell so fresh and clean. I have often said I wish I could can and market puppy smell.

Over the years I have had numerous dogs and currently have a miniature Dachshund. Notice I stated I have, because I don't own Pettie; he resides at my current address. You see, most Dachshunds are very independent and possessive, my little guy is no exception.

If you lived in Biblical times your concept of a dog would be entirely different. Dogs were owned to be watchdogs and were considered predators. Some were domesticated for the care of sheep, but people who were disliked were compared to vicious dogs. Note! There is an old saying that a dog comes back to what he has vomited, and a pig is washed only to come back and wallow in the mud again. That is the way it is with those who turn again to their sin.

They make these proverbs come true: "A dog returns to its vomit, and a washed pig returns to the mud."

(2Peter 2:22 NLV)

There are numerous other verses that depict how odious dogs were to the masses.

Matthew records an incident of the mindset about dogs and of what our Lord thought about canines.

A Canaanite woman from that vicinity came to him, crying out, 'Lord, Son of

David, have mercy on me! My daughter is suffering terribly from demon possession.' He replied, 'It is not right to take the children's bread and toss it to their dogs.'

(Matthew 15:22-26)

Her reply, "Yes, Lord,' she said "but even the dogs eat the crumbs that fall from their master's table."

(Matthew 15:27)

Dogs were tolerated, but they were not the cuddly animals we have come to love. Was our Lord insensitive about animals? I don't believe He was, but He was using a principle to teach us about faith. The woman was half Jew and half Gentile, shunned by the Jewish populace because they were considered worse than dogs. For Christ to even talk to her would have been construed by the religious leaders as a sin. He met her need at that moment and rewarded her for her faith. She lowered herself as a lowly dog, true humility. Her daughter was delivered from demon possession and a soul was restored to fellowship with God.

Our little dog has given my wife and I much joy for the short time we have had him, but he has taught me some kingdom principles that have helped me better understand God's creatures.

Genesis states:

And God said, 'Let the land produce living creatures according to their kinds; livestock, creatures that move along the ground, and wild animals, each according to its kind,' and it was so. God made the wild animals according to their kinds, the livestock according to their kinds, and all the creatures that move along the ground according to their kinds. And God saw that it was good.

(Genesis 1:24-25)

Dogs can be a great comfort to us who are dog owners, but as stated above, my little dog has shown me how dependent I am on God in my life.

Let me give you an illustration. I generally take my canine for a walk each day. I must use a leash when I take him for his walk. His leash is the only way I can control him. The leash is sixteen feet long and is a retractable type.

One of the things he has learned is he can only go as far as the leash will allow him. He has this habit of looking back at me when I pull the retractor; it's as if he is saying to me why can't I go any farther? It is like when we reach the end of our boundaries God has placed on us. He says to us, "Dear child, don't go any farther or you are going to get hurt." Sound familiar? Like my little dog's leash, I keep him from running out into the street so he can't get hurt. God gave us the Holy Spirit to keep us from getting hurt.

My dog depends upon me to feed and house him; I, as a Christian, exercise my faith and I am dependent on Christ for my needs. A small dog brings a lot of joy to my wife and me. He sometimes eats the crumbs that fall from my table and at times I feed him scraps. He knows that I love him, just as I know God loves me. Not because He feeds me, but because He died for me, therefore I am dependent on Him.

If you are a dog owner, next time a scrap falls from the table and your dog snatches the crumb, remember the Canaanite woman that was asking for only the crumbs that Jesus could give her in her time of need.

And my God shall supply all your needs according to his riches in glory in Christ Jesus.(Philippians 4:19 NASB)

Chapter Seven

Keeping in Step

There is no wisdom, no insight, no plan that can succeed against the Lord.

(Proverbs 21:30)

If you are like me, I am sure you have made certain plans for your life that didn't work out the way you wanted them to.

When I was a young man all I wanted to do in life was to be a professional baseball player. I dreamed of being a major league pitcher. I could quote to you the earned run averages of all the great super stars of the day. How many games they had won and lost? I slept and ate baseball.

After I finished high school, I was fortunate to play a few years in the minor leagues, until I developed shoulder problems which ended my career. I found myself with barely a high school diploma and virtually no profession or skills that would help me procure a decent job. My plans were founded on dreams rather than being guided by God. A scripture that comes to mind is "The steps of a good man are ordered by the Lord: and he delighted in his way" (Psalm 37:23 KJV). People who have no relationship with God live at times by impulse rather than by a clear direction from the Lord. This is the way I lived my life rather than ask God for guidance. I assumed this was what I was supposed to do.

Reflecting back on my early years I can see the errors I made.

Unfortunately, others are affected by the wrong choices we make, usually family and friends.

I remember a young man who had all the potential in the world as an athlete. I first met him playing semi-professional baseball in Southern California. He was a tall,

lanky individual, six feet five in stature and could throw the baseball as hard as anyone in the game. He had all the potential and natural ability a man could desire. He had several flaws in his personal makeup that would haunt him the rest of his life. He was sought after by every major league scout of his day.

Two of his major flaws were that he like to party and drink and he did not take life seriously. He was a clown and was always playing practical jokes.

One night in a bar his would come crashing down around him. He and another fellow ballplayer were drinking and after consuming several adult beverages they became inebriated. They met another patron in this bar and something snapped in Blackie, he and the other fellow proceeded to beat the other man to death. They were charged with murder, convicted, and sent to prison for life. Blackie had built his plans and dreams and wishes which came tumbling down.

This story did not have a happy ending; he was to spend the next twenty years in a California State prison. He became the best pitcher in prison and is considered a legend by the other inmates. When he was finally released, he signed a contract with a team in the Pacific Coast League. Far beyond his prime, and all for the wrong choices he made.

This is a true story, and a tragic one because this man in his impetuous youth took a life and I venture to say a day didn't go by that he wasn't sorry for his actions. Man-made plans and dreams are just that, but when a person follows his dreams and not God's plans they generally fail.

My own life somewhat parallels Blackie's life. Other than spending life in prison, I worked hard and pursued worldly dreams without God's leading. I achieved most of my dreams, but there was something missing in my life – Jesus Christ.

In his heart a man plans his course, but the Lord determines his steps.

(Proverbs 16:9)

Christ had other plans for my life and he revealed them to me when I asked him to come into my heart. As the psalmist states, our plans start in our hearts, but it's God who directs them.

In Him we were also chosen, having been predestined according to the plan of him who works out everything in conformity with the purpose of his will.

(Ephesians 1:11)

A man's steps are directed by the Lord. How then can anyone understand his own way?

(Proverbs 20:24)

These two verses are very special to me, because I could have followed my own dreams rather than God's plans. I often wonder whatever happened to Blackie, it's been over fifty years since I last saw him. I don't know if he is even alive, but give the opportunity to ask him one question, I would ask, "Would you live your life over if given another chance?" I believe his response would be, "Without a doubt."

When we ask Christ into our lives, He gives us another chance to live our lives guided by Him. How about you? Are you living life guided by your emotions, or is God the one who directs your path? It's your choice.

Chapter Eight

Salt of the Earth

Season all your grain offerings with salt. Do not leave the salt of the covenant

Of your God out of your grain offerings; add salt to all your offerings.

(Leviticus 2:13)

One of my favorite programs on television is the History Channel. One such program that caught my attention was a special that focused on what was happening to the great pyramids.

The problem is people. In a hot climate people perspire and perspiration contains salt that the body releases through the process of perspiring. The salt that humans emit is causing the hieroglyphics to deteriorate. They have to close these great artifacts from the populace in order to preserve them. The program showed the great pains being undertaken in order to maintain these great national treasures. Installing humidifiers was one of the many devices being used to stop the erosion. Meanwhile experts are meticulously scraping the salt from the walls.

These great monuments were preserved for thousands of years while they were sealed, but once they were opened to the public they started to erode, caused by the salt that secretes from our perspiration, how ironic.

As I watched this special my thoughts turned to what Jesus said:

You are the salt of the earth. But if the sale loses its saltiness, how can it be made salty again? It is no longer good for anything, except to be thrown out and trampled by men.

(Matthew 5:13)

I thought how tragic that salt is a preservative, yet in this instance the very thing that preserves was destroying what is left of a great society that once ruled the earth.

Salt is used for many purposes in our lives. As humans we need salt in our daily diets to maintain a healthy body. Too much salt in your diet can affect your blood pressure, which in turn causes you heart problems.

The first time I went to Minnesota was to be at my granddaughter's wedding. While coming out of a restaurant, my eye caught a sight I had never seen before. I noticed a car's bumpers and fenders bouncing up and down. As I examined this strange aberration, I noticed that the fenders and bumpers were tied together with bungee cords. My grandson explained to me that the fenders and bumpers were tied to the car's chassis due to the rust caused by the salt used during the winter months, to keep cars from sliding all over the icy winter roads.

Thus, salt has its good qualities and in certain climates it helps save lives. If you live in the mid-west during the winter months it helps keep you safe on the winter roads. The adverse effect is it deteriorates your car by rusting. People who live near the ocean can expect the same results, since salt water causes metal to rust.

If you live in Israel near the Dead Sea you can swim in a sea that has buoyancy, some claim it has medicinal attributes. We have the same type of sea here in the United States, in the state of Utah call the Great Salt Lake. Then we have the great Bonneville Salt Flats; where cars are tested for their endurance and speed.

A dentist will recommend that you wash your mouth with warm salt water to help heal a tooth extraction. A doctor will prescribe that you gargle with warm salt water if you have a throat infection.

When Jesus referred to us as the salt of the earth, He was saying that salt if a good symbol of God's activity in a person's life, because it penetrates, preserves, and aids in healing.

In Arab countries, an agreement was sealed with a gift of salt to show the strength and permanence of the contract. Believers are call "the salt of the earth" (Matthew 5:13). Let the salt you use remind you that you are one of God's covenant people. We are to help preserve and purify the world.

I started this with what is happening to the pyramids because of salt from humans. We can season the world with the salt of the Gospel and live our lives as Christ directed us. Or we can become tasteless and not fit for anything. I close with the words of Jesus, "Salt is good, but if it loses its saltiness, how can it be made salty again? It is fit neither or the soil nor for the manure pile; it is thrown out." "He who has ears to hear, let him hear" (Luke 14:34-35)

Chapter Nine

Building the Kingdom

Unless the Lord builds the house, its builders labor in vain.

(Psalm 127:1a)

One of the myths of Christianity is that His kingdom is being built solely by men and women in full time ministry. Not so; God's kingdom is built up by all the members of His body.

Much energy, time and money are spent in furthering God's kingdom. Denominations recruit and send missionaries to all parts of the globe. Foreign countries are inundated by hundreds of men and women who have pledged their lives to the furtherance of the gospel. They all arrive in these countries with great expectations, believing they all have the right answers in order to spread the good news.

The same happens here in our own country when we send out local missionaries. When their great expectations are not met, they feel deserted and lonely, broken and saddened that the call they felt they had on their lives must have been a mistake. Some even drop out of fellowship, bruised and battered.

Sad, but true, the story above is a reality for some. Full-time ministry can at times be disheartening, I know and have felt the despair that can come with failure. One of the problems is that as humans we are never taught to fail. We hear of all the success stories of people with gigantic ministries, so when people fail in establishing a church or a successful ministry, they can't handle failure.

We can apply the same principle to all of life. Unless God is the focal point of a family the house is being built on expectations. House is symbolic of God's family. In today's society we see families being torn apart by divorce, their dreams and expectations built on whims rather than on the promises of God.

Paul writes:

If any man builds on this foundation using gold, silver, costly stones, wood, hay, or straw, his work will be shown for what it is, because the Day will bring it to light. It will be revealed with fire, and the fire will test the quality of each man's work. If what he has built survives, he will receive his reward.

(I Corinthians 3:12-14)

This verse speaks of advancing the Kingdom of God, but I think we can apply it to individuals and families since the church of Christ is made up of all believers.

With all of the distractions in our culture and society it is difficult to stay focused on building the church of God. Yet when I read this verse that states it is God who builds His house, in modern terms we are spinning our wheels. Ministries try all sorts of programs, even gimmicks, to try to lure people into their respective churches, yet, sad to say, they fail.

What I think is needed more than anything today is to hear the voice of the Holy Spirit as in the Book of Acts.

While they were worshiping the Lord and fasting, the Holy Spirit said, 'Set apart for me Barnabas and Saul for the work to which I have called them.'

(Acts 13:2)

This verse has two mandates: one, prayer and fasting and second, it is God the Holy Spirit that selects people for full time ministry.

We must pool our resources and work together in order to further the gospel.

Unless the Lord builds the house, its builders labor in vain.

(Psalm 127:1a)

Let God be the focus of our prayers and let God build His kingdom. We who have been gifted to serve in full time ministry are blessed. But it takes the entire body of Christ working for the same goal, let God build his house. Amen!

Chapter Ten

Hearing the Master's Voice

Come, follow me, Jesus said, and I will make you fishers of men.

(Matthew 4:19)

I can't imagine how many articles and sermons have been written or preached about the words of Jesus when He said, "Come, follow Me and I will make you fishers of men" (Matt. 4:19). I have thought long and hard about these words. I have visualized our Lord walking by the Sea of Galilee and what His thoughts were when He saw these man mending their nets.

As Jesus was walking beside the Sea of Galilee, he saw two brothers, Simon called Peter and his brother Andrew. They were casting a net into the lake, for they were fishermen.

(Matthew 4:18)

Going on from there, he saw two other brothers, James, the son of Zebedee and his brother John. They were in a boat with their father Zebedee, preparing their nets. Jesus called them.

(Matthew 4:21)

What amazes me is that without hesitation the two disciples "At once they left their nets and followed him" (Matt. 4:20). What command and authority He showed as they left everything to follow our Lord? He didn't promise His disciples riches, or fame, but that they would reach humans.

They understood the principle of fishing, but the Master knew how to reach to the very core of their souls. We must understand that in Christ's day life was harsh, it was demanding just to survive in the Roman controlled world. Something in Jesus' voice had a sense of urgency. The Master was walking among His creation calling them to a new way of life.

The Sea of Galilee is a large lake. Roughly 30 fishing towns surrounded the lake during Jesus' day, Capernaum being the largest.

Jesus was calling them away from their productive trades to be productive spiritually. We all need to fish for souls. If we practice Christ's teachings and share the gospel with others, we will be able to draw those around us to Christ, like a fisherman who pulls fish into his boat with nets.

These men already know Jesus. He had talked to Peter and Andrew previously (John 1:35-42) and had been preaching in the area. When Jesus called them, they knew what kind of man he was and were willing to follow him. They were not in a hypnotic trance when they followed but had been thoroughly convinced that following him would change their lives forever. When we accept Christ as our Savior, in essence we become fishers of men.

They saw in Christ a hope for the future that would change their lives of servitude to a life serving Him. As they continued to learn from Him, the more it became evident that they were called to serve.

I have never been one who loves to fish, but I know enough about the type of fishing they were accustomed to doing. It was hard, grueling, tedious work. They started early in the morning and worked well into the late evening. Pulling and casting the nets that were very heavy when they were empty, imagine when they were full of fish the weight they had to pull. How does this tie into catching people? The principle is that the ministry of catching people requires hard work and dedication.

Jesus had a plan in the area of bringing people into the kingdom. He used men who were used to hard work, wo were not afraid to dedicate their lives to the work He had called them to.

Ironically people still fish in the same manner in some o the third world countries, casting nets the same way as their ancestors did in the time of Christ. Commercial fishermen use nets in our country, but the main difference is that they use motors t o haul the nets into their boats. Still, it is hard demanding work.

Being fishers of men today is no different than in Christ's time; the method may have changed, but God is saying I want you to catch men and women. I want you to fulfill the great commission.

Then Jesus came to them and said; all authority in heaven and on earth has been given to me. Therefore, go and make disciples of all nations, baptizing them in the name of the Father and of the Son and of the Holy Spirit, and teaching them to obey everything I have commanded you. And surely, I am with you always, to the very end of the age.

(Matthew 28:18-20)

Churches have all sorts of programs and classes on how to evangelize their communities, towns, and cities. Based on the principles that Jesus taught they are the same today, but I think we have to use different methods.

There are millions throughout the world who have never read or heard the gospel. We have been given a mandate by God to reach the lost.

Jesus said:

I am sending you out like sheep among wolves. Therefore, be as shrewd as snakes and as innocent as doves.

(Matthew 10:16)

Christ came to save us from eternal damnation, we can make a difference. Jesus is still saying to us:

Come, follow me, Jesus said, and I will make you fishers of men.

(Matthew 4:19)

Chapter Eleven

Surfing the Waves

I made the sand a boundary for the sea, an everlasting barter it cannot cross.

The waves may roll, but they cannot prevail; they may roar, but they cannot cross it.

(Jeremiah 5:22b)

One of the sports that I have always been fascinated by is surfing. Once I was privileged to watch a surfing tournament at one of the Southern California beaches. What intrigued me was the way the surfers would wait to catch a specific type wave in order to score points.

As I watched the men sit astride their boards waiting to catch the perfect wave, I was fascinated by how the men who were competing would catch their wave and ride the wave to a certain point. All this by balancing themselves on the board as they glide on the top of the wave, riding the crest as it glides towards shore.

This to me is what surfing is all about: catching the perfect wave, ride it as far as you can, then drop off and wait for the next wave. As I continued to observe this phenomenon I thought about Jesus while in a boat with His disciples:

He got up, rebuked the wind and said to the waves, 'Quiet! Be still!' Then the wind died down and it was completely calm.

(Mark 4:39)

Can you imagine our Lord in today's society watching men surf? Especially calming the waves; the one thing a surfer lives for. I don't believe they would be too pleased with Him for spoiling their passion if He calmed the ocean as they surfed.

While Jesus was asleep in a boat the sea became choppy with huge waves. Wakened from a sound sleep, He calmed the tempest because of the fear the disciples were experiencing. Surfers live on the edge. To them the bigger the wave the greater the high and exhilaration, for us who don't surf, getting caught in a big wave could challenge our faith as it did the disciples.

Surfing requires a certain type of person. It is a sport that demands a lot of patience and a faith in your own abilities. As you drive along the California coast on any given day you will see men and women sitting astride their boards waiting for the right wave, dressed in their wetsuits, their ankles tied to the board, looking for the perfect wave.

I remember as a youth one of the things we did during the summer months was to go to "Tin Can Beach." Today it is called "Huntington Beach" and we did our own version of surfing. We called it body surfing, similar to what they do with the great boards they use today. The main difference in those days was the degree of the waves and how far out we would swim. It did not require the ability to balance your self, like today. But there was a degree of risk, yet not as dangerous as today's surfing. It was really dangerous if you got caught in a rip tide. Many people have drowned over the years due to rip tides. When you are young and adventurous you are more apt to put caution aside.

Once I caught a wave that I almost drowned in. I think I swallowed half the Pacific Ocean, but the next day I was back doing the very thing that the previous day had almost one me in. It was my youth and my lack of fear that made me continue to return to body surfing.

What can we learn from all this? Life for some is like a surfer looking for the big wave to ride, trusting in one's own abilities, rather than in God. When a surfer gets knocked off his board he gets right back on, waiting for the next wave. In one respect we need to be more like a surfer when we go through a trial. Get back on the board of life, go into the deep water and ride the waves.

The Psalmist writes:

Trust in the Lord with all your heart and lean not on your own understanding; in all your ways acknowledge him, and he will make your paths straight.

(Proverbs 3:5-6)

A surfer must swim out a certain distance to catch a specific wave, at times through turbulent rough water. He must trust in his ability and what he has learned about surfing.

We as Christians need to trust God and not in our abilities, but in His word to guide us. When the big waves of life hit us, then we can ride on top. The Holy Spirit will bring us the balance we need and carry us to shore. Like a surfer with patience waiting for the big wave we can wait on God to see us through any and all tests.

There are people who live their lives like a novice surfer. The never learn to ride a wave. Like the disciples in the boat with Jesus they constantly cry out whenever any size wave upsets their life. They have a very shallow faith.

The Bible states that:

...faith cometh from hearing, and hearing by the word of God.

(Romans 10:17 KJV)

An experienced surfer will practice his skills. He has gone through many failures in obtaining a level of excellence. As Christians we will go through many trials.

Paul writes:

Not only so, but we also rejoice in our sufferings, because we know that suffering produces perseverance; perseverance, character, and character, hope.

(Romans 5:3-4)

Life will always have trials, but Jesus will always be in the boat with us to calm us and the waters and, like Peter, when we get out of the boat, we have to trust God to keep us afloat, riding the crest of life.

Chapter Twelve

The Early Fig

Now learn this lesson from the fig tree; As soon as its twigs get tender and its leaves come out, you know that summer is near.

(Matthew 24:32)

One of my favorite fruits is figs. Once we lived in a home that had a fig tree along with an orange tree. Both of my trees produced fruit. The orange tree is of the Navel variety. I haven't a clue as to what type of figs my tree produced. All I know is that it produced an abundance of fruit. People you ask in my part of the country don't care for tree-ripened figs. Respond by saying they prefer the dried variety.

I remember when we first moved into this home how much I like figs and could hardly wait for my tree to produce its yearly crop. When early summer arrived, there were hundreds of buds on my tree, but no figs. One day while working in the yard I spotted a lone purple fig. I reached up and picked that one fig and proceeded to eat the first early fig. It was like honey to my mouth. I can still taste the sweetness of that lonely ripe fig. It would be several weeks before my tree would produce any more edible figs. It would be late fall in my part of the country and I still had a tree with ripe figs, and a messy yard full of rotting figs that the birds had partially eaten or had fallen to the ground, only to rot.

I remember as I ate the lonely fig what Jesus must have been looking for when He approached a fig tree.

Early in the morning, as he was on his way back to the city, he was hungry. Seeing a fig tree by the road, he went up to it but found nothing on it except leaves. Then he said to it, 'May you never bear fruit again!' Immediately the tree withered.

(Matthew 21:18-19)

In another instance Jesus told a parable about a fig tree.

Then he told this parable: 'A man had a fig tree, planted in his vineyard, and he went to look for fruit on it, but did not find any. So, he said to the man who took care of the vineyard, For three years now I've been coming to look for fruit on this fig tree and haven't found any. Cut it down! Why should it us up the soil? Sir, the man replied, leave it alone for one more year, and I'll dig around it and fertilize it. If it bears fruit next year, fine! If not, then cut it down.'

(Luke 13:6-9)

In these two passages of scripture are two great illustrations of producing fruit in the believer. The cursing of the fig tree was a lesson to his disciples about faith. He went on and explained to His disciples about moving mountains, based on faith. Some have claimed that He was cursing the nation of Israel because they rejected Him as Messiah. The second parable was spoken about the nation of Israel being given a second chance to repent of its sins and recognize Him as Messiah.

There is a great principle to learn from both illustrations. We as Christians are to produce fruit in our lives to further the kingdom of God. The parable touches my heart when I see people who have made a commitment to Christ and never see any fruit in their lives. Each time I reach up and pick a ripe fig I am reminded of these two scriptures.

Jesus used another parable using the fig tree allegorically, He told them this parable:

Look at the fig tree and all the trees. When they sprout leaves, you can see for yourselves and know that summer is near. Even so, when you see these things happening, you know that the kingdom of God is nearby.

(Luke 21:29-31)

The fruit of the fig tree was part of the staple diet of the Israelites. They understood what Jesus was saying when He told them to compare the leaves of the fig tree in comparison to His second coming.

Some of the Old Testament prophets give us great illustrations, using figs as examples of Biblical prophesy. Jeremiah the prophet states:

One basket had very good figs, like those that ripen early; the other basket had very poor figs, so bad they could not be eaten. Then the Lord asked me, "What do you see Jeremiah?" "Figs," I answered. "The good ones are very good, but the poor ones are so bad they cannot be eaten."

(Jeremiah 24:2-3)

What a great illustration pertaining to the types of fruit believers produce, versus non believers. The best fruit of the fig tree is the early fruit. Later in the season the fruit loses its sweetness. The late figs are left on the tree and eventually fall off and rot. The figs start to rot while still on the tree.

Dried figs were a staple food in Biblical times. I personally like dried figs and could probably eat a pound at one setting by myself. A few years ago, my wife and I were blessed to go to Spain for our vacation. One of the side trips of our trip was to visit the British colony of Gibraltar.

While touring the various shops I went into a produce shop and spotted a bin full of dried figs. I purchased a few pounds so that I could take them with me on the plane trip home.

When we boarded the plane, I had my stash of dried figs tucked away in my carry-on bag. During the eight-hour flight I took out the bag of figs and ate a few of the delicious figs. About the time I bit into my third or fourth fig, the flight attendant announced that all fruit had to be eaten or disposed of. I ate a couple more figs and threw away a couple pounds of my prized figs. After we were told we would be landing in a few minutes, I asked the attendant about dried fruit. To my chagrin I was told dried fruit could pass through customs. It was too late to retrieve my figs, which had been collected and thrown away.

Like is either like ripe sweet figs or the dried variety. One life is squandered and self serving it is thrown away. It cannot be retrieved. Giving your life to Christ can be like Jeremiah stated, "the good ones are very good" (Jeremiah 24:2a). It is our choice as to the type of fruit we become, good or bad. If you are not a fig eater next time you go to your local grocery store, pick up the fresh kind or the dried type. Whichever you choose you won't be disappointed; prayerfully it will remind you of the passage in Jeremiah. "The good ones are very good" (Jeremiah 24:2a). Perhaps you will reflect on where you are in your walk with Christ.

Chapter Thirteen

Light Bulbs Come in All Sizes

In the same way, let your light shine before men, that they may see your good deeds and praise your Father in heaven.

(Matthew 5:16)

Thomas Edison is given credit for the invention of the electric light bulb. I don't know how many times he failed in his quest to find the right elements in order to succeed. Even though he failed time after time, and at times he became discouraged, yet he knew that he would eventually persevere if he stayed his course. After his numerous failures, he was asked how he felt about his discovery. His reply was that he now knew thousands of ways how not to make a light bulb.

His commitment led to a discovery that would change the course of history. Like the printing press, his endeavors would help revolutionize the industrial world. Because of Edison they built great hydroelectric plants and harnessed great rivers to produce electricity for the world; all because he had a vision to harness electricity. He had a vision to light up the world. He succeeded because of his ability to stick to his goal and vision.

Jesus said:

You are the light of the world. A city on a hill cannot be hidden. Neither do people light a lamp and put it under a bowl. Instead, they put it on its stand, and it gives light to everyone in the house.

(Matthew 5:14-15)

If Thomas Edison had discovered the electric light bulb only for his personal use, he would have been a very shallow individual. It would be like placing your lamp under the bed. We are not to hide what we have been give, our salvation. Our light is a reflection of the Son, the Lord Jesus Christ. It is His light in us that is to light up the hearts of mankind.

Today is you go to buy a light bulb you will be confronted with a display of every type and size bulb imaginable. There are clear bulbs, night lights, refrigerator bulbs, one for your stove and even one that comes on by movements called a sensor bulb. You even get three-way bulbs, some 75, 150, 300 watts. Some of us are like a three-way bulb or a refrigerator bulb, we can turn our brightness on and off or our light goes on only when we turn it on like the refrigerator bulb, when we open the door.

You can even install a dimmer switch to dim you lights to a glow. There are Christians who have a built-in dimmer switch, or are like the three-way bulb. Jesus wants us to shine our light all the time, not when it suits us. One of the most tragic things to happen is to turn your light off completely.

The psalmist says:

The Lord is my light and my salvation, whom shall, I fear? The Lord is the stronghold of my life, of whom shall I be afraid?

(Psalm 27:3)

John writes about Jesus being the light:

When Jesus spoke again to the people, he said, "I am the light of the world. Whoever follows me will never walk in darkness, but will have the light of life."

(John 8:12)

This is the message we have heard fro him and declare to you: God is light; in him there is no darkness at all.

(I John 1:5)

Since God is light and if He truly lives in us, then the light will shine upon others. "In the same way, let your light shine before men, that they many see you good deeds and praise your Father in heaven" (Matt. 5:16). I leave you with one thought, are you a high intensity bulb, or are you one of those three-way bulbs, or perhaps your bulb has burned out? Or is your light the type you can control the wattage as well as the intensity? Our light should be like a beacon, shining bright and calling others to the true light, Jesus Christ.

Chapter Fourteen

Grace With Age

Even when I am old and gray, do not forsake me, O God, till I declare your power to the next generation, your might to all who are to come.

(Psalm 71:18)

Having worked as a hospital chaplain, in a hospital that had an extended care facility for the elderly, I was always amazed at the care they received. Seniors who are debilitated require a lot of extra care in a hospital and an extended care facility meets their needs in most cases.

Recently I went to a gathering of retired ministers and those who were over 65 years of age. I thought about how far we have come as Christians when we look forward to retirement. I do not believe that the Bible states we should look to retirement when we reach a certain age in life.

I think of Moses when he was told by God:

Go up into the Abraum Ranges to Mount Nebo in Moab, across from Jericho, and view Canaan, the land I am giving the Israelites as their own possession. There on the mountain that you have climbed you will die and be gathered to your people, just as your brother Aaron died on Mount Hor and was gathered to his people.

(Deuteronomy 32:49-50)

Moses had served the Lord for 40 years leading the Israelites in the wilderness, but when they were about to enter into the Promised Land God told him he was to die on Mount Nebo. God hadn't promised him a savings account or stocks, but he was promised leadership of a nation, the nation of Israel.

Based on scripture and as David the psalmist states:

Even when I am old and gray, do not forsake me, O God, till I declare your power to the next generation, and your might to all who are to come.

(Psalm 71:18)

David was crying out to God to let him always be a witness for Him, to share the love and mightiness of God, the God who chose him to establish the lineage of Messiah.

I as a senior citizen resent when young people look down on the elderly, as if we don't have something to give.

Job states:

Is not wisdom found among the aged? Does not long-life bring understanding?

(Job 12:12)

A life lived serving God can be an asset to the church. We need to tap into one of God's greatest resources, the aged. Our legacy lies in what those who went before us learned and passed down to those of us who follow. I feel saddened when I see older pastors and the elderly set aside, with no longer a voice, full of wisdom going to waste.

Science has made it possible with the help of God to lengthen the life span of people. Men and women are living longer and longer with the advances that modern medicine has discovered. Yet I see men and women set aside for the younger when they still have much to offer.

David writes:

Do not cast me away when I am old; do not forsake me when my strength is gone.

(Psalm 71:9)

If you are a senior citizen, have you ever prayed as David prayed? Perhaps you have lost your mate and feel rejected by God. Don't despair – He has not forsaken you and you are still important to God.

Proverbs states:

Gray hair is a crown of splendor; it is attained by a righteous life.

(Proverbs 16:31)

Paul wrote in his first letter to the Corinthians the importance of each member of God's body.

Now the body is not made up of one part but of many.

(1 Corinthians 12:14)

Further in the passage he states:

On the contrary, those parts of the body that seem to be weaker are indispensable, and the parts that we think are less honorable we treat with special honor. And the parts that are unpresentable are treated with special modesty.

(I Corinthians 12:22-23)

We are to honor the elderly and hold them in high esteem. All the parts of the body are important to God. Some of the people I respect the most are those who have lived serving God well into their eighties.

Fanny Crosby, who wrote the hymn "Blessed Assurance," wrote into her nineties and died at the ripe old age of 96, truly a great saint.

The psalmist put it so succinctly when he wrote:

Young men and maidens, old men and children. Let them praise the name of the Lord, for his name alone is exalted; His splendor is above the earth and the heavens.

(Psalm 148:12-13)

We need to focus on the one who alone deserves our adoration, the Lord Jesus Christ. He cares for us all and desires us to be in unity. When I see the elderly with no hope or joy, they need to know that Jesus holds them in high esteem, truly set apart.

God didn't take into consideration how old Moses was when He called him. Both Aaron and Moses were 83 and 80 respectfully when He called them to be His spokesmen. They were comfortable in their surroundings, in their lifestyles, but they obeyed the call.

David says:

With long life will I satisfy him and show him my salvation.

(Psalm 91:16)

Isaiah writes:

I will be your God through all your lifetime, yes, even when your hair is white with age. I made you and I will care for you. I will carry you along and be your Savior.

(Isaiah 46:4 NLT)

Amen!

Chapter Fifteen

More Precious Than Gold

The crucible for silver and the furnace for gold, but the Lord tests the heart.

(Proverbs 17:3)

Have you ever noticed how some of us humans react when we are shown gold or gold jewelry? Our eyes light up, entranced by what glitters as well as its monetary value.

One of my all-time favorite movies is "Treasure of Sierra Madre." It was filmed many years ago and stars Humphrey Bogart and Walter Huston, the father of the famous director, who directs the movie. The setting takes place in the mountains of the state of Durango, Mexico in the late 1920's. Three drifters meet in a flop-house and decide to join up to hunt for gold. They set us for the Sierra Madre mountains in search of the elusive metal.

The plot thickens when they discover gold, but the discovery uncovers their real characters. Humphrey Bogart plays a psychotic who feels that the other two men want to steal his share. Through an accident to an Indian child in the area the three are separated. Dobbs, played by Bogart, thinks the other man is trying to kill him so he in turn shoots his partner. Thinking he has killed his partner he leaves him for dead and takes off with the gold to Durango. On the way he is killed by bandits. The bandits think that the gold in the sacks in plain sand to add weight to the burros in order to sell them. They cut all the sacks and spill all of the gold. The wind comes and blows all the gold away.

Eventually the other two men get to Durango and find out what happened to their partner and the gold. The movie ends with the two laughing at what has transpired. A great line ends the scene, with Walter Huston stating, "I don't know if fate has dealt us a hand or the good Lord had the last laugh, anyway the gold is blown by the wind back to where it came from."

The moral is they were fools to think they could cheat God. Haggai the prophet puts it so succinctly.

The silver is mine and the gold is mine, declares the Lord Almighty.

(Haggai 2:8)

Gold, as mentioned in the Bible, like today had tremendous value. Wars were fought for this elusive mineral. Kingdoms were divided in order to control the economy. Excavations of the great pyramids uncovered great fortunes buried with the Pharaohs for them to us in their concept of the next world.

Isaiah writes:

I will make man scarcer than pure gold, rarer than the gold of Ophir.

(Isaiah 13:12)

This verse is part of the judgment prophesied against Babylon. The gold of Ophir was a rare gold, desired by most of the populace. Numerous other passages of scripture speak of gold. Things have not changed since biblical times as to the desire for gold, a measure of worldly wealth.

Peter and John were on their way to the temple for prayer when they encounter a beggar who is lame. Peter, looking at this ragged creature, is moved by the Holy Spirit and recognizes that the man could be restored to wholeness.

Then Peter said, 'silver or gold I do not have, but what I have I give you. In the

Name of Jesus Christ of Nazareth, walk.'

(Acts 3:6)

Many of us look upon our circumstances as being victimized and that we have certain rights due to our plight. This man was looking for monetary help. God supernaturally intervened and healed him, not for gold or silver, but in order to further His kingdom.

What transpired next is great when you see his reaction to his miraculous healing.

He jumped to his feet and began to walk. Then he went with them into the temple courts, walking and jumping, and praising God.

(Acts 3:8)

There are times when God wants to bless us in very insignificant ways. This man was thinking he was going to get money, silver or gold, instead he received a life to serve

God.

He refined this man to a life of holiness and service.

Peter writes:

In this you greatly rejoice, though now for a little while you may have had to suffer grief in all kinds of trials. These have come so that your faith of greater worth than gold, which perishes even though refined by fire may be proved genuine and may result in praise, glory and honor when Jesus Christ is revealed.

(I Peter 1:6-7)

As I understand this passage of scripture our faith is more important than gold. The analogy is that our faith, like gold which is refined, is refined by the trials of life.

The movie story I shared is a great example of being test by fire. In life there are no shortcuts to riches. There aren't any shortcuts to God's eternal kingdom and salvation. We must be first tested by fire. An old saying states, "All that glitters is not gold." Life is full of God's nuggets; we need to be sensitive spiritually when we are going through a testing; it could turn out to be one of God's blessings.

One of the greatest lines ever uttered in a movie is found in this movie. The three men encounter a band of bandits. Dobbs asks the leader of the banditos if he is a federalist. And where is your badge to prove who you say you are? The bandit replies, "Badges? I don't need to show you no stinking badges." This line has been quoted over and over for many years, but I think sometimes people are like the bandit, we think we don't need to show our faith.

It takes intense heat to purify gold and silver. Similarly, it often take the heat of trials for the Christian to be purified. Through trials, God shows us what is in us and clears out anything that gets in the way of our complete trust in Him. Trials of life will come your way, realize that God wants to use them to refine your faith and purify your heart like refined gold.

Chapter Sixteen

Lost and Found

For this son of mine was dead and is alive again; he was lost and is found. So, they began to celebrate.

(Luke 15:24)

Have you ever lost an article of value, perhaps a piece of jewelry, or even the keys to your car? Maybe you lost the house keys and became frantic when you couldn't find them. I venture to say that most of us have experienced some loss of such an item. Did you feel joy and relief when you found the lost article? Of course, you did, it's a natural emotion.

Year ago, my wife and I went to Spain and while we were there, I purchased a man's pinky ring. I really loved that ring because it was a memento and a reminder of a great trip. It was also special due to the fact that my grandparents were from Spain and our plans were to visit the place of their birth.

I was to lose this gold ring two times, ironically both times while playing golf. The ring was Spanish Gold with a Lapis lazuli stone setting. The first time I lost the ring was due to a habit I had of taking the ring off because it hindered my golf grip. I would place the ring in my golf bag and at the end of my round would replace the ring on my finger.

This one particular time without thinking about the ring, I dropped the golf cart and bag in a small pond and without my knowledge the ring fell out of the bag. Much to my chagrin I discovered my loss when I arrived at home. I was frantic because of the sentimental value of the ring. I remembered the next day about dropping the cart at the edge of the pond and retraced my steps and there to my great joy was the ring glittering at the edge of the water. The elation and joy that I felt was my good fortune in finding my lost ring. Sad to say I lost the ring a few years later in Mexico while playing a round of golf. I searched to no avail for my elusive treasure; I even hired some young boys to search for my lost ring, my precious treasure was gone forever.

As I reflect on this incident in my life, I think about the three parables our Lord taught in the Gospel of Luke, found in chapter fifteen. There are three great illustrations of lost souls. The first one talks about the good shepherd that leaves the 99 in safety and goes after the one gone astray.

And when he finds it, he joyfully puts it on his shoulders and goes home. Then he calls his friends and neighbors together and says,' Rejoice with me; I have found my lost sheep.'

(Luke 15:5-6)

Note that the lost sheep is carried by the shepherd, this is our Lord who carries our loads, our sins; each and every indiscretion we have committed and ever will, is carried by our Savior.

The second parable speaks of a woman who loses a coin.

Or suppose a woman has ten silver coins and loses one. Does she not light a lamp, sweep the house and search carefully until she finds it? And when she finds it, she calls her friends and neighbors together and says, "Rejoice with me; I have found my lost coin.

(Luke 15:8-9)

As I see this parable our Lord was using a hook of sorts. His audience was made up of tax gatherers and so-called sinners who dealt with money. The coin was equivalent to a day's wages. Jesus understood their minds. He spoke to the very thing they valued the most, money.

Again, the theme is the value of something that is lost and the joy when it is found. Joy of something lost then found here on earth and in heaven is the bait:

In the same way, I tell you, there is rejoicing in the presence of the angels of God over one sinner who repents.

(Luke 15:10)

Remember Jesus is speaking to sinners, those who needed a Savior.

This parable is one of the greatest parables of rejoicing found in the Bible. The young man had squandered his fortune and was lost in sin. Jesus was making a point about the rejoicing that goes on in heaven when a person who is a sinner comes to his senses. The young man comes to his senses because he recognizes that he is a sinner.

The Father never gave up on the lost son as He states:

But while he was still a long way off, his father saw him and was filled with compassion for him; he ran to his son, threw his arms around him and kissed him.

(Luke 15:20)

Love and forgiveness awaits the lost repentant sinner.

The love that God our heavenly Father has for the lost cannot be measured by our standards, but we get a glimpse of His love and grace. Note:

But the father said to his servants, "Quick! Bring the best robe and put it on him. Put a ring on his finger and sandals on his feet. Bring the fattened calf and kill it. Let's have a feast and celebrate.'

(Luke 15:22-23)

All of us are sinners and are lost until we recognize we need a Savior who will guide us throughout our lives. Those who ask Christ to come into their hearts are assured an eternal place where rejoicing will be eternal. You are worth more than gold or silver to God. The entire message of being lost and then found is how much God loves the sinner.

Are you in need of a Savior? He is waiting for you. The great hymn "Amazing Grace" states it so well. "Amazing grace, how sweet the sound that saved a wretch like me, I once was lost but now am found." Amen!

Chapter Seventeen

Road Signs

Enter through the narrow gate. For wide is the gate and broad is the road that leads to destruction, and many enter through it. But small is the gate and narrow the road that leads to life, and only a few find it.

(Matthew 7:13-14)

Whenever my wife and I plan a trip to a place we are unfamiliar with, we take out the area map of the town or city we are planning to visit and plan our trip accordingly. Most of us who go on vacation or plan an outing do the same. Even when we reach our destination, we look for the proper road signs or the name of the street we have in mind. I'm sure it has happened to many of us. Even with all the directions and well-made plans we sometimes take the wrong turn or wind up in the wrong section of town.

Why are the choices we make in our lives; at times seem like we took the wrong turn or didn't read the road signs carefully enough? Or perhaps we ignored the vital signs altogether and have lived our lives on impulse, or what we feel at the moment.

If we do the latter we are living on the edge and are in for some rough times. Great disappointments and emotional hurts await us, all because we took the wrong turn of life.

Jesus said:

Enter through the narrow gate. For wide is the gate and broad is the road that leads to destruction, and many enter through it. But small is the gate and narrow the road that leads to life, and only a few find it.

(Matthew 7:13-14)

You might ask, what are the road signs and road maps of life? I look to God's word as the road map. It give us clear precise direction found in the scriptures. Like we learn to read a road map we must learn how to read the Bible.

It states in one of the Psalms:

Show me your ways, O Lord, teach me your paths.

(Psalm 25:4)

We must allow God to teach us and be sensitive when He directs our paths.

For this God is our God for ever and ever; He will be our guide even to the end.

(Psalm 48:14)

Scripture is very clear that God directs the righteous if we submit to Him.

We as Christians are road signs to others. We are to point and give directions to the lost by how we live our lives. When we say we are believers our lives must reflect the one who made it possible, the Lord Jesus Christ.

Christians can give the wrong type of directions by their actions, either good or bad. Younger people watch us to see how we live our lives to either follow or go their own way.

I would ask myself and you; what type of a road sign are you? Are you one that states danger, caution dangerous curve ahead, or perhaps your sign reads; slow down, bumpy road ahead.

A great illustration concerning signs happened to me. A few years ago, I damaged my knee to a point that necessitated two surgeries. As a result, I was given a disability by a court-appointed doctor and give a special sign. This placard allows you to park in designated spaces for the handicapped.

Once I parked in a handicapped space and forgot to place the placard in a visible place in my vehicle. When I returned to my car there was a fine assessment of several hundred dollars. I was at fault because of my lapse of memory. I didn't pay attention to the sign that said; caution you must have a proper valid handicapped placard to park in this specially designated parking space.

Can I blame the state for my actions? No, but I can mediate the fine, which I did. We as Christians have a mediator, Jesus Christ, when we don't heed the signs and fall into the temptations of life. He forgives us because He paid the penalty for us on the cross.

The greatest sign to mankind is the cross of Christ, it points the way to salvation. It is an eternal sign for all of mankind.

Chapter Eighteen

Behind Closed Doors

Here I am! I stand at the door and knock. If anyone hears my voice and opens the door, I will come in and eat with him, and he with me.

(Revelation 3:20)

Have you ever noticed how important doors are in all societies? Most of us would never think of buying or renting a home without doors. The most important reason we have doors is for privacy. Even people who live in the deserts in tents have some sort of flap or covering that serves as a door.

Every building, home, or edifice has some sort of entrance; a pair of massive swinging doors or sliding doors. And some, revolving types. Their purpose is to give you access into the structure. It serves as an entrance or exit. When you get inside the building you will find other doors to various rooms.

In a home you will find doors leading to all sorts of rooms, the bedroom, or the bathroom, or perhaps into a study. Even closets have doors. You will find sliding doors leading to the outside patio, or the backyard. If you live in an apartment there will most likely be a door leading to a balcony or patio. All these doors have some sort of lock to keep you safe from intruders or for your privacy. We place locks on our bedroom doors as an added precaution for privacy. At night when we retire to go to sleep, we make sure that the deadbolts and locks are secured and in place both on the front and back doors.

In some neighborhoods the people have bars on their windows for added safety and security, to keep people out. Families move to gated communities in order to feel secure and have a sense of privacy.

Even our modes of transportation have security locks on the doors. They are installed to give the person who is driving the vehicle a feeling of safety and security. We even have seatbelt laws to make us more secure.

Prisons are built with doors to keep the inmates from escaping as well as to let the guards in and out.

When early man lived in caves, it was for their protection, but they also built a sort of door at the entrance to keep other tribes from raiding their dwellings. They also

placed guards at the entrance as an added protection.

Doors also serve another purpose, they help keep the cold, rain, and snow outside of the building during the winter months, and in the hot seasons they help keep the temperature down.

Biblical times were no different than those of today.

People gathered inside their homes and close their doors for security and safety, for the same reasons people do today, behind close doors for the same reasons we do, for privacy and safety. "Door" is often used in figurative senses in the Bible. In the Old Testament, "sin is crouching at your door."

(Genesis 4:7)

Means that sin is very near. The valley of Anchor, a place of trouble (Joshua 7:26), is later promised as "a door of hope" (Hosea 2:15). It will become a reason for God's people to trust Him again.

In the New Testament Jesus calls Himself "the door" (John 10:7; John 10:9). Faith in Him is the only way to enter the kingdom of God. God gave the Gentiles "the door of faith," or an opportunity to know Him as Lord (Acts 14:27). Paul constantly sought a "door of service," an occasion for ministry in the name of Christ (I Corinthians 16:9).

Jesus stands at the door and knocks (Revelation 3:20). He calls all people to Himself, but will not enter without our permission. The ironic thing about this passage is that Jesus is talking to the believers, the church at Laodicea. Note!

I know your deeds, that you are neither cold nor hot. I wish you were either one or the other!

(Revelation 3:15)

It is tragic when the Master stands at the door of a believer's heart and has to knock at the door of our heart to let Him in.

As Christians we can become so hardened in our hearts that God isn't allowed to do the sculpting in our hearts. God has many ways of molding and shaping us into the image of His Son.

The psalmist writes:

Do not harden your hearts as you did at Meribah, as you did that day at Massah in the desert.

(Psalm 35:8)

These locations were a time of great testing for the Israelites under the leading of Moses. Sometimes we react to adversity wrongly and close our hearts to what Jesus wants to do. The door of our heart must always be open to the Master.

Chapter Nineteen

Mountain Climbing

The mountains melt like wax before the Lord, before the Lord of all the earth.

(Psalm 97:5)

Several years ago, I had the pleasure of meeting the first man to conquer Mount Everest, Sir Edmond Hillary. I remember I asked him why he had attempted such a great challenge when others before him had been turned back in failure. I remember his answer was not a patented answer, but a genuine belief: "Because it was there."

I have often thought of his comment and why anyone would risk their life for the sole purpose of achieving greatness and notoriety. Another man reached the pinnacle of the world's highest mountain on that same day, Tensing Norkem\ay, a Sherpa guide. Most people remember Hillary, but few remember Tensing.

Other have conquered Everest since that day over half a century ago. Many have died on the freezing slopes of the world's highest point. Thousands have been turned back in failure, due to the extreme cold and adverse weather conditions. Many return to try again," because it's there."

Life is like climbing the world's highest mountain with all its adversity, but with one huge difference, Christ is with us through all life's adversity, its trials and tribulations. Jesus went to the mountain on several occasions. Once He took three disciples with Him. They were blessed beyond their dreams. They saw Moses and Elijah, two prophets of old who had climbed the mountain of God. Moses received the Law and saw a portion of God's glory. Elijah heard the soft voice of God when he felt all alone. Peter, John and James saw Christ transfigured before their eyes and heard the voice of the Father. Perhaps those who attempt to climb their mountains are seeking God.

I believe there are some who seek to get close to God by climbing other mountains, look for Him in the wrong places. The Nation of Japan has its mount Fuji; a holy place to the millions of Buddhists who try to climb it once in their lifetimes.

The Incas worshiped in the Andean mountains, seeking their God. The Muslims make an annual pilgrimage to worship God at Mecca. The current temple of the Muslim faith sits on the site where Solomon's temple flourished, the center of Jewish worship. The city of Jerusalem is built on a hill called Mount Moriah where Abraham offered up Isaac, later called Mount Zion.

Man is always looking for God in the high places, maybe it's a carry over from the Israelites when God spoke to them from Horeb as they wandered in the wilderness and where Moses received the laws of God.

Jesus said a unique thing in His dialogue with the woman at the well, when He declared:

Believe me, woman, a time is coming when you will worship the Father neither on this mountain nor in Jerusalem. You Samaritans worship what you do not know; we worship what we do know, for salvation is from the Jews. Yet a time is coming and has now come when the true worshipers will worship the Father in spirit and truth, for they are the kind of worshipers the Father seeks. God is spirit, and his worshipers must worship in spirit and in truth.

(John 4:21-24)

We are not to look for God in the heights nor depths, but in our hearts.

Many of us go to retreats seeking a closer relation with God, but have we not learned what the master was saying? Elijah look for God in all the wrong places until God got his attention. God's voice over-shadowed Moses' and Elijah's presence on the Mount of Transfiguration when His voice thundered. Peter asked Jesus if he could build three shrines for each of them.

While he was still speaking, a bright cloud enveloped them, and a voice from the cloud said, 'This is my Son, whom I love; with him I am well pleased. Listen to him?'

(Matthew 17:5)

We are to focus our desires and dreams with Christ at the center of them. Climbing mountains may satisfy a desire to accomplish some sort of goal in life, but the real challenge is to live our lives for the Lord. Seeking Him daily, the mountains of life are difficult enough without seeking fulfillment in false mountains.

The Jews heard the voice of God coming from the Holy Mountain. If you don't know Jesus, are you still searching for an encounter with God on your mountain? Ask Him to come into your life in the privacy of your home, in the innermost part of your soul and that hunger will be satisfied.

It requires faith in Him as He said:

I tell you the truth, if anyone says to this mountain, 'Go, throw yourself into the sea,' and does not doubt in his heart but believes that what he says will happen, it will be done for him.

(Mark 11:23)

He is there. Amen!

Chapter Twenty

"Greco Roman Style"

For we wrestle not against flesh and blood, but against principalities, against powers, against the rulers of the darkness of this world, against spiritual wickedness in high places.

(Ephesians 6:12 KJV)

Paul, being a Roman citizen and most likely having seen the Olympic style games as a boy, alludes to the Roman and Greek athletic games in several of his writings. The word "struggle," or as the K.J. version states, "wrestle" is a word that expresses the thought of the Greek wrestling matches. The closest English word we have that expresses this term is the word "struggle."

The "Games" to the Greek and Romans were a daily part of their lives.

Paul writes:

And also, is anyone competes as an athlete, he does not win the prize unless he competes according to the rules.

(2 Timothy 2:5)

Years ago, as a young man, at the expense of the United States Army,

I had the privilege of serving in Japan. While I was there, I went to see a Sumo wrestling match. To this day I don't have a clue as to what the purpose of this style of wrestling is, other than that tie is brute strength against brute strength. They charge at each other to knock the opponent out of a small ring, the person who does this is declared the winner.

Here in the United States and Mexico millions of people annually attend the so-called wrestling matches, to watch muscular behemoths entertain their audiences. These men are very gifted athletes and in tremendous shape in order to perform their skills. There is some semblance of the original intent, but over the years it has evolved into billions of dollars as an industry.

On rare occasions a participant will injure himself, but because these matches are choreographed and the outcome prearranged, this it is entertainment, nothing more. There are people who believe that this so-called sport is real. That the combatants are really out to hurt each other, but most people know this form of wrestling is entertainment, nothing more.

The book of Genesis tells us that Jacob wrestled with a man all night.

Then Jacob was left alone, and a man wrestled with him until daybreak. And when he saw that he had not prevailed against him, He touched the socket of his thigh; so, the socket of Jacob's thigh was dislocated while he wrestled with him. Then he said, let me go, for the dawn is breaking. But he said, I will not let you go unless you bless me. So, he said, what is your name? And he said, 'Jacob." And he said, Your name shall no longer be Jacob, but Israel; for you have striven with God and with men and have prevailed.

(Genesis 32:24-28 NASB)

Jacob had wrestled with an angel of God, but because he prevailed, God changed his name to Israel. This passage of Scripture also states that Israel limped as a sign that he had wrestled with God.

When Paul the apostle wrote the book of Ephesians and stated that our life struggle is not against the things we can see, but that we are in a spiritual battle.

For our struggle is not against flesh and blood, but against the rulers, against the authorities, against the powers of this dark world and against the spiritual forces of evil in the heavenly realms.

(Ephesians 6:12)

Each time I read this verse I get a mental image of life as a gigantic wrestling match and the struggles and trials are preparing us for future battles, battles we will win because of what Jesus did at Calvary.

Paul writes:

Therefore, put on the full armor of God, so that when the day of evil comes, you may be able to stand your ground, and after you have done everything, to stand.

(Ephesians 6:13)

These are the weapons we are to use to overcome the spiritual battles we will fight in life. All of life's struggles are not spiritual, but there is an evil force that would deter you from the course that God has set for each of His saints. Like the wrestling shows watched, that are choreographed, some of life's trials are such when we disobey God. The challenge to us is to know when we are fighting a spiritual battle.

One of the greatest spiritual battles being fought today is for the survival of the traditional family and the minds o9f our children. The bombardment we see in the television and movie industry of the deviant sexual lifestyles as a choice, rather than what it really is, blatant sin.

The music that many of our young people listen to today is a spiritual battle for the minds of our children.

Parents and families are under attack daily, in our schools in what our children are allowed to learn and what they are being taught. These are the real battles being fought today. The sad part is many of our parents are losing the battle because they are spiritually unaware of what is going on around them.

Jacob wrestled with God and prevailed because of his faith and the promises of God. The full armor of God is made up of defensive weapons, not offensive weapons. Our greatest offensive weapon is prayer.

The Book of Hebrews states:

Therefore, since we have so great a cloud of witnesses surrounding us, let us also lay aside every encumbrance, and the sin which so easily entangles us, and let us run with endurance the race that is set before us.

(Hebrews 12:1 NASB)

We are to run life's race according to the rules that are set before us, and we will prevail.

If you are struggling with your faith.

Fight the good fight of the faith. Take hold of the eternal life to which you were called, when you made your good confession in the presence of many witnesses.

(I Timothy 6:12)

Amen!

Chapter Twenty-One
Needed Foot Washing

So, he got up from the meal, took off his outer clothing, and wrapped a towel around his waist. After that, he poured waster into a basin and began to wash his disciples' feet, drying them with the towel that was wrapped around him.

(John 13:4-5)

Years ago, before I became a Christian, my wife and I went to a county fair in Southern California. I remember as I entered the fairgrounds, I was greeted by a Catholic priest who was handing out New Testaments. I remember I jokingly stated since they were free, I would take two. He graciously gave me the two Bibles. I took them home and placed them next to my bed in as drawer.

One night a few weeks later I remembered the testament and decided to read it. I remember I started with the Gospel of John. It was to be my first attempt at reading the Bible. I remember when I started to read the thirteenth chapter I began to weep. My thoughts were really confused so I immediately dropped the Bible and placed it in the night stand. I thought if He was really God, how could God stoop so low to wash the feet of mere men. This passage haunted me for several months. I never picked up a Bible again until Christ came into my heart months later.

This passage is one of the greatest examples of servanthood expressed in the entire Bible. I have often thought what humanity and Christianity needs today is people who are willing to serve. The world stresses that we should take care of ourselves first Jesus showed a principle of more than serving, but in order to further His kingdom we must be willing to become slaves.

It was just before the Passover Feast. Jesus knew that the time had come for him to leave this world and go to the Father. Having loved his own who were in the world, he now showed them the full extent of his love.

(John 13:1)

The passion of His love for them drove Him to express His love in doing something that was relegated to the poorest servant or slave. Note Peter's indignation:

"No," said Peter, "you shall never be my feet." Jesus answered, "Unless I wash you, you have no part with me." "Then, Lord." Simon Peter replied, "not just my feet but my hands and my head as well!"

(John 13:8-9)

What a sight this must have been to the disciples. The teacher, the master, stooping so low as to gird a slave's towel around His waist and assume the role of a slave and then proceed to wash and wipe their feet. A kingdom principle was established, if God came to earth to serve mankind as an example, is there any task that we as Christians are not to do?

When I read this passage, I think of the thousands who work in retirement homes who must take care of the aged. People who work with the disabled who cannot do for themselves what a healthy normal person can do. I think of those who care for patients in hospitals who rely on the nurses and staff to care for their daily needs.

Often when I read this passage of scripture, I reflect back on my first encounter with the Holy Spirit the night I wept and thought how could God lower Himself and take on the role of a slave. That night the Holy Spirit started the process of my conversion.

Jesus expresses His heart in the balance of the passage:

For I give you an example that you also should do as I did to you. Truly, truly, I say to you, a slave is not greater than his master; neither is one who is sent greater than the one who sent him. If you know these things, you are blessed if you do them.

(John 13:15-17 NASB)

Our washing and cleansing is a continuum, it is a process that goes on daily in our lives. It is the pruning, the conviction the Holy Spirit does in the life of the believer. At times we don't like the pulling and the stretching, but God wants us to produce good fruit.

Most of us wash our fruit prior to eating to clean off the dirt or pesticides. Jesus was teaching and dealing with pride. His example addressed the problem wit the religious leaders of the day, pride. By His humbling act, He was saying you can't serve Me is you are prideful. Pride and arrogance go hand in hand, because prideful people are self serving and generally have only themselves in mind.

The Marine Corps motto states, "We are looking for a few good men." The Army had as their motto, "Be all you can be." Christianity should have a motto, "Serve to the Fullest."

Are you looking to serve, maybe you should learn how to wash feet, it can be a humbling experience?

If you know these things, you are blessed if you do them.

(John 13:17 NASB)

Chapter Twenty-Two

"Father to the Fatherless"

Fathers, do not exasperate your children; instead bring them up in the training and instruction of the Lord.

(Ephesians 6:4 NIV)

Working as a marriage and family counselor along with being a full-time minister, I am exposed to and come in contact with; many different types of fathers. Many of the ones that I see in my practice have various issues concerning their role as a parent and father. With the growing number of absentee fathers at pandemic proportions, it is no wonder children of today have a difficult time relating to the concept of a "Loving Father."

I think back to the type of father my earthly father was. He was a good man and worked hard all of his life to raise eight children. Others state that they see some of Dad in me, and I feel a sense of pride when I hear a relative make this statement. My father had flaws like all of us, overall, he was a man of integrity and honesty, a great virtue that is lacking in many men today. I greatly admired this in my father; he taught all of his sons this principle, by the way he lived his life.

My father as far as I can remember, never told us the importance of having a deep relationship with Jesus Christ. I don't fault him for this, because he was raised by his mother and barely knew his father. When Paul the Apostle wrote his letter to the church at Ephesus, he was setting a great principle to all future fathers in how to raise their children.

As children we learn from our parents, by their role playing. Fathers live and set examples to their children. Paul clearly sets three great principles for us to model.

And fathers, do not provoke your children to anger; but bring them up in the discipline and instruction of the Lord.

(Ephesians 6:4 NASB)

The first is provoking a child to anger. We can provoke a child by our mood swings. If we are angry and frustrated all the time, your child over a period of time will think this is the norm and you will see a child with an aggressive personality.

The second principle is crucial in understanding the word "discipline." This word comes from the Latin word "disciple." We fathers are literally disciplining our children, especially our sons. A student learns from his teacher, either good or bad. Jesus taught this principle to his disciples when he washed their feet. He was the master, yet He was willing to lower Himself as a slave to show us a principle of role modeling.

The third principle and vital to the spiritual health of our children is teaching them the virtues and direction for their lives. Far too many fathers want the wife to teach their children the words of God, or they rely on the local church to teach them the concepts of the scriptures, when

God's word states very clearly it is the father's responsibility.

I am saddened that I was not able to teach my sons the importance of God. We only get one chance at raising and teaching our children. One of my passions as a minister is teaching young men how to be good fathers, men who can provide a place of security and an environment of nurturing their children in the ways of God.

Paul, in writing to the Corinthian church, wrote;

For if, you were to have countless tutors in Christ, yet you would not have many fathers; for in Christ Jesus, I became you father through the gospel.

(I Corinthians 4:15 NASB)

I believe God always gives us a second change to rectify errors we make in life. In my case it was a case of ignorance, since I did not know the Lord until my children were almost grown, but I think of the men who know better, yet fail to raise their children in the knowledge of our Lord Jesus Christ.

God is God to the fatherless and will always seek ways for us to be a father image to some young men or women. A young child who yearns for the love and male bonding only a Godly man can provide. One of my favorite passages of scripture is the story of the prodigal son. The father had two sons; one went and squandered all of his inheritance on loose living. The older one stayed at home, but held resentment for his brother when the brother repented and came and asked forgiveness of his father. The father welcomed him and asked his servants to prepare a banquet in honor of the lost son.

Scripture states that when the father called all of his servants to make preparations for the party, the older son became angry with the father; but the father's response was,

And he said to him, 'My child, you have always been with me, and all that is mine is yours. But we had to be merry and rejoice, for this brother of you was dead and has begun to live, and was lost and has been found.'

(Luke 15:31-32 NASB)

I believe that men of God are called to be fathers to the fatherless. There are many children who go to bed at night who have never felt the love of an earthly father, let alone a heavenly Father. If you are reading this page and are being led by the Holy Spirit to be a surrogate father, then follow His leading. Maybe you are one of those men whom I called absentee fathers, or an overbearing father. You may even be the abusive type of father. Why not be the father God wants you to be, one who knows how to love and discipline according to God's Word, it takes a commitment on your part. As they say in today's vernacular, go for it. Amen!

www.ingramcontent.com/pod-product-compliance
Lightning Source LLC
Chambersburg PA
CBHW041130110526
44592CB00020B/2759